Gianfranco Ravasi

Abraham
FATHER OF OUR FAITH

ILLUSTRATED BY Silvia Colombo

PAULIST PRESS
New York / Mahwah, NJ

Of the many wonderful and treasured episodes of the Bible, the story of Abraham is among the most beautiful in the entire Judeo-Christian tradition. In this story, God promises Abraham a place to live and a long-awaited son— and Abraham puts his trust in him.

The Letter to the Hebrews says, "By faith Abraham obeyed when he was called to set out for a place that he was to receive as an inheritance; and he set out, not knowing where he was going. By faith he stayed for a time in the land he had been promised, as in a foreign land, living in tents" (11:8–9).

A long journey
through history

Now these are the descendants of Terah. Terah was the father of Abram, Nahor, and Haran; and Haran was the father of Lot. Haran died before his father Terah in the land of his birth, in Ur of the Chaldeans. Abram and Nahor took wives; the name of Abram's wife was Sarai, and the name of Nahor's wife was Milcah. She was the daughter of Haran the father of Milcah and Iscah. Now Sarai was barren; she had no child.

Terah took his son Abram and his grandson Lot son of Haran, and his daughter-in-law Sarai, his son Abram's wife, and they went out together from Ur of the Chaldeans to go into the land of Canaan; but when they came to Haran, they settled there.

The days of Terah were two hundred five years; and Terah died in Haran.

(Genesis 11:27–32)

Abraham's story is told in the first book of the Bible, Genesis, from the end of the eleventh chapter to the beginning of the twenty-fifth. It begins with the description of the family of Terah whose sons were "Abram, Nahor, and Haran."

In the above passage, a difficult word is used: *genealogy*. Genealogy means "the study of the origins of a family or the study of all the people who descended from the same ancestor." The Book of Genesis tell us that Terah descended from Shem, who was one of Noah's sons.

In this way, the Bible tells us that the story of Abraham takes place within a long line of people in the history of humanity. The list of fathers and sons is not just a boring sequence of names; instead, it's a beautiful way of connecting history. This shows us that God—in his goodness—never abandons people. And God chooses Abraham to fulfill a special promise for all people.

Noah

Shem

Terah

Haran

Nahor

Abram

Haran

Canaan

Ur

8

Terah is from Ur of the Chaldeans—a wealthy city in southern Mesopotamia founded four thousand years before Christ. From there, he leaves for a long journey toward the land of Canaan, taking his son, Abraham, his daughter-in-law, and his grandson. Biblical scholars believe this journey took place more than 1,700 years before Jesus was born.

The family stops and stays for a while in Haran—an important stopover point for trading caravans from rich cities. Terah dies there without ever reaching his goal. But we shall see that his son, Abraham, does not give up. God himself will give him the strength to continue toward his father's ultimate goal, the land of Canaan—the promised land of God.

Go forth from your country

Now the LORD said to Abram, "Go from your country and your kindred and your father's house to the land that I will show you. I will make of you a great nation, and I will bless you, and make your name great, so that you will be a blessing. I will bless those who bless you, and the one who curses you I will curse; and in you all the families of the earth shall be blessed."

So Abram went, as the Lord had told him; and Lot went with him. Abram was seventy-five years old when he departed from Haran. Abram took his wife Sarai and his brother's son Lot, and all the possessions that they had gathered, and the persons whom they had acquired in Haran; and they set forth to go to the land of Canaan.

(Genesis 12:1–5)

Here the most beautiful part of Abraham's story begins—when he was seventy years old. The Bible says he is a wealthy cattle breeder who moves through the territory of Haran with his flocks of animals and his tents. Still today, the inhabitants of the Arabian Peninsula and North Africa—called Bedouin tribes—live in much the same way: they migrate based on the seasons and move their tents where there are better pastures.

This is how Abraham is living when God chooses him. God calls him and says to him, "Go forth from your country…" And Abraham responds in obedience: "So Abram went, as the LORD had told him." Abraham trusts completely and unconditionally. He does not ask questions, nor does he seek signs or confirmations from God. Instead, he departs and leaves behind his country, his kindred, and his father's house.

14

In these verses of Scripture, the word *bless* is used five times:
"I will bless you; you will be a blessing. I will bless those who bless
you; and in you all the families of the earth shall be blessed." Through
Abraham, all the nations of the earth will be blessed. Abraham does
not choose things as a privilege only for himself; instead, the mission
is entrusted to him for the good of all people. And when someone sets
out with joy, that joy becomes a blessing for all those who are near.

15

God promises Abraham a new land

The LORD said to Abram, after Lot had separated from him, "Raise your eyes now, and look from the place where you are, northward and southward and eastward and westward; for all the land that you see I will give to you and to your offspring forever. I will make your offspring like the dust of the earth; so that if one can count the dust of the earth, your offspring also can be counted. Rise up, walk through the length and the breadth of the land, for I will give it to you." So Abram moved his tent, and came and settled by the oaks of Mamre, which are at Hebron; and there he built an altar to the LORD.

(Genesis 13:14–18)

17

When he finally reaches the land God showed him, God makes Abraham a great promise: "I will give you and your descendants all the land that you see, forever. I will make your descendants like the dust of the earth." God promises him a place where he will live—the land of Canaan. It refers to the present as well as to the future; in other words, the promise is not only for Abraham, but it is for everyone who will come after him—his descendants.

In the ancient world, having descendants (that is, children) was considered a sign of God's blessing. The opposite—not having children—was considered a curse. Abraham is childless, but he continues living as a nomadic shepherd with the hope of having descendants as numerous as the dust or as the sand of the sea and the stars of heaven (later metaphors that will be used).

Abraham will have to wait a long time, but along the way, he receives signs that God is with him and will never forget his promise.

God promises
Abraham descendants

After these things the word of the LORD came to Abram in a vision, "Do not be afraid, Abram, I am your shield; your reward shall be very great." But Abram said, "O Lord GOD, what will you give me, for I continue childless, and the heir of my house is Eliezer of Damascus?" And Abram said, "You have given me no offspring, and so a slave born in my house is to be my heir."

But the word of the LORD came to him, "This man shall not be your heir; no one but your very own issue shall be your heir." He brought him outside and said, "Look toward heaven and count the stars, if you are able to count them." Then he said to him, "So shall your descendants be." And he believed the LORD; and the LORD reckoned it to him as righteousness. Then he said to him, "I am the LORD who brought you from Ur of the Chaldeans, to give you this land to possess."

(Genesis 15:1–7)

The great promise of God to be Abraham's "shield" seems impossible: Abraham is an old man and he is still childless. By now, he has already appointed his servant, Eliezer from Damascus, to be his heir. In Abraham's day, when someone had no children, they usually appointed a servant or a slave to inherit all their possessions. And it was Eliezer who had the responsibility of taking care of his adoptive parents in their old age.

But Abraham receives a sign of hope. One starry night, God asks him to go outside his tent and look up at the sky above him: his future descendants will be counted as the number of the stars.

Abraham has to choose whether to trust God and his word. He has no doubts, and he believes. In the Hebrew language, the verb *to believe* leads to another word, *Amen* (with which we finish our prayers). It means "to lean on or to trust." Abraham trusts in God and puts himself and his future in God's hands. His act of faith is received with joy by God. It is the most beautiful thing Abraham can give and the most wonderful offering God can receive from anyone: people's trust.

The covenant and the
announcement of
the birth of
a son

When Abram was ninety-nine years old, the Lord appeared to Abram, and said to him, "I am God Almighty; walk before me, and be blameless. And I will make my covenant between me and you, and will make you exceedingly numerous."

Then Abram fell on his face; and God said to him, "As for me, this is my covenant with you: You shall be the ancestor of a multitude of nations. No longer shall your name be Abram, but your name shall be Abraham; for I have made you the ancestor of a multitude of nations. I will make you exceedingly fruitful; and I will make nations of you, and kings shall come from you. I will establish my covenant between me and you, and your offspring after you throughout their generations, for an everlasting covenant, to be God to you and to your offspring after you. And I will give to you, and to your offspring after you, the land where you are now an alien, all the land of Canaan, for a perpetual holding; and I will be their God."

God said to Abraham, "As for Sarai your wife, you shall not call her Sarai, but Sarah shall be her name. I will bless her, and moreover I will give you a son by her. I will bless her, and she shall give rise to nations; kings of peoples shall come from her."

Then Abraham fell on his face and laughed, and said to himself, "Can a child be born to a man who is a hundred years old? Can Sarah, who is ninety years old, bear a child?" God said, "No, but your wife Sarah shall bear you a son, and you shall name him Isaac. I will establish my covenant with him as an everlasting covenant for his offspring after him."

(Genesis 17:1–8, 15–17, 19)

Abrah

God returns once again to speak to Abraham. Again, he renews the promises he has already made. But this time, he connects the promises to a covenant with Abraham's descendants: he will be the God of all people who descend from Abraham—forever. And as a symbol of this change, Abraham—who up until now had been called *Abram*—receives a new name: *Abraham*. His name means "father of a multitude." The same thing happens to his wife. Before, she had been called *Sarai*; but now she, too, receives a new name: *Sarah*.

Changing one's name in the ancient eastern world represented a change of destiny and calling. Abraham and Sarah, friends of God, now begin a great new journey as the people God will use to show his love to the entire world.

Abram

Despite their old age and Abraham's confusion as he falls down laughing before God, the Lord promises once again that they will have a son. The son's name will be a permanent remembrance that Abraham had laughed at God's promise and that God had laughed at his two friends' disbelief. In fact, his name, *Isaac*, means "God laughs."

The mysterious visit of the three men

The LORD appeared to Abraham by the oaks of Mamre, as he sat at the entrance of his tent in the heat of the day. He looked up and saw three men standing near him. When he saw them, he ran from the tent entrance to meet them, and bowed down to the ground. He said, "My lord, if I find favor with you, do not pass by your servant. Let a little water be brought, and wash your feet, and rest yourselves under the tree. Let me bring a little bread, that you may refresh yourselves, and after that you may pass on—since you have come to your servant." So they said, "Do as you have said."

And Abraham hastened into the tent to Sarah, and said, "Make ready quickly three measures of choice flour, knead it, and make cakes." Abraham ran to the herd, and took a calf, tender and good, and gave it to the servant, who hastened to prepare it. Then he took curds and milk and the calf that he had prepared, and set it before them; and he stood by them under the tree while they ate.

They said to him, "Where is your wife Sarah?"
And he said, "There, in the tent." Then one said,
"I will surely return to you in due season, and your wife
Sarah shall have a son." And Sarah was listening at the
tent entrance behind him. Now Abraham and Sarah were old,
advanced in age; it had ceased to be with Sarah after the manner of
women. So Sarah laughed to herself, saying, "After I have grown old,
and my husband is old, shall I have pleasure?" The LORD said to Abraham,
"Why did Sarah laugh, and say, 'Shall I indeed bear a child, now that I am
old?' Is anything too wonderful for the LORD? At the set time I will return to
you, in due season, and Sarah shall have a son." But Sarah denied, saying,
"I did not laugh"; for she was afraid. He said, "Oh yes, you did laugh."

(Genesis 18:1–15)

Now an amazing event takes place within the desert tent. Abraham has settled with his tribe by the oaks of Mamre in the area of Hebron. The Bible tells of a mysterious meeting.

Three men, sent by God, appear before Abraham's tent. Abraham speaks to them as if they were just one person. In the Christian tradition, these three people have been described as angels, and they are interpreted as a symbol of the Trinity.

The Book of Genesis describes Abraham's generous hospitality, which is typical of how people treated their guests in the ancient eastern world. Abraham acts quickly and urgently. So does Sarah, who goes to work immediately. Even the servant quickly slaughters a tender calf. The entire story is full of energy and movement. Bread cakes, beef, yogurt, and fresh milk are sumptuously laid before the guests who are seated at the table. Abraham—who was seated at the beginning of the story—now stands in consideration of his guests and ready to serve them.

During the meal, the three men explain why they are there. God has once again returned to proclaim the promise of a son.

But Sarah is too old to have children and she does not believe in the message they received: "In due season Sarah shall have a son." According to the custom then, she is not allowed to sit with the men at the table, so she stands at the entrance to the tent. She stands ready to serve and tries to understand why those three mysterious guests are there. When she hears their words, she "laughs." At this point, the men question her disbelief: "Is anything too wonderful for the LORD?" they ask. Sarah tries to deny that she had smiled because of her human doubt. Like Abraham, she laughs because of her unbelief.

The birth of Isaac

The LORD dealt with Sarah as he had said, and the LORD did for Sarah as he had promised. Sarah conceived and bore Abraham a son in his old age, at the time of which God had spoken to him. Abraham gave the name Isaac to his son whom Sarah bore him. Abraham was a hundred years old when his son Isaac was born to him. Now Sarah said, "God has brought laughter for me; everyone who hears will laugh with me." And she said, "Who would ever have said to Abraham that Sarah would nurse children? Yet I have borne him a son in his old age."

The child grew, and was weaned; and Abraham made a great feast on the day that Isaac was weaned.

(Genesis 21:1–3, 5–8)

Sarah is "visited" by the Lord of life. Even though she is sterile and her husband is an old man, she has a son whom they name *Isaac*. The Book of Genesis carefully explains the name given to the child, Isaac. It comes from the Hebrew word *sahaq*, and means laughter, joy, or dancing. The disbelieving "laugh" of Sarah and Abraham is changed into the "smile of the Lord" who has kept his promise.

43

Isaac grows up. When he arrives at the age of weaning (the age when babies stop nursing), Abraham celebrates with a great feast. We can imagine what it was like: surely there was much dancing, joy, happiness, and laughter. This was typical in large families and tribes at such occasions.

The celebration described here after such a long wait for the fulfillment of God's promise of a child is very important. But, as we will see, it does not last. Abraham's faith will soon be harshly tested, and the rest of his journey will be very difficult.

God puts Abraham to the test

After these things, God tested Abraham. He said to him, "Abraham!" And he said, "Here I am." He said, "Take your son, your only son Isaac, whom you love, and go to the land of Moriah, and offer him there as a burnt offering on one of the mountains that I shall show you." So Abraham rose early in the morning, saddled his donkey, and took two of his young men with him, and his son Isaac; he cut the wood for the burnt offering, and set out and went to the place in the distance that God had shown him. On the third day Abraham looked up and saw the place far away. Then Abraham said to his young men, "Stay here with the donkey; the boy and I will go over there; we will worship, and then we will come back to you."

Abraham took the wood of the burnt offering and laid it on his son Isaac, and he himself carried the fire and the knife. So the two of them walked on together.

Isaac said to his father Abraham, "Father!" And he said, "Here I am, my son." He said, "The fire and the wood are here, but where is the lamb for a burnt offering?" Abraham said, "God himself will provide the lamb for a burnt offering, my son." So the two of them walked on together. When they came to the place that God had shown him, Abraham built an altar there and laid the wood in order. He bound his son Isaac, and laid him on the altar, on top of the wood. Then Abraham reached out his hand and took the knife to kill his son. But the angel of the Lord called to him from heaven, and said, "Abraham, Abraham!" And he said, "Here I am." He said, "Do not lay your hand on the boy or do anything to him; for now I know that you fear God, since you have not withheld your son, your only son, from me."

And Abraham looked up and saw a ram, caught in a thicket by its horns. Abraham went and took the ram and offered it up as a burnt offering instead of his son. So Abraham called that place "The LORD will provide"; as it is said to this day, "On the mount of the LORD it shall be provided."

(Genesis 22:1–14)

In these terrible pages, God tests Abraham over what he holds most dearly. The story is very difficult to understand. It begins by saying, "Take your son, your beloved son Isaac, whom you love, and…offer him there as a burnt offering!" Then everything goes silent. In the same way as he left Ur and Haran, Abraham does not say anything; instead, he goes forth with his son, his two servants, a donkey, and a load of wood for the holocaust. A holocaust was a burnt offering of a living person who had to be completely consumed in the fire. Some followers of ancient religions sometimes practiced this. The offering is now Isaac, whom Abraham must first kill and then burn.

51

The dramatic journey lasts three days and is completely silent. Isaac breaks the strange silence only when they arrive at the foot of the mountain in "the land of Moriah." He is tender and innocent as he questions his father, "Father!" "Here I am, my son!" responds Abraham. "The fire and the wood are here, but where is the lamb for the burnt offering?" asks Isaac. Abraham responds, "God himself will provide the lamb for the burnt offering, my son!" We feel Abraham's pain in their dialogue, but we also sense his trust in God who appears cruel and confusing.

When they reach the top of the mountain, Abraham begins the solemn preparation for the awful ritual practiced by nearby religions. These rituals were called "foundational sacrifices." When someone built a city or a palace, he would kill his firstborn son on the very site where he was about to build. They believed that such offerings would appease the gods, who would, in turn, offer them protection. Child sacrifices—often performed while worshiping the Phoenician god, Moloch—were rare.

The command of God—who until now had presented himself as the Lord who loves and gives life—is even more striking. But Abraham obeys in complete and pure faith. Like a priest, he builds an altar, gathers wood, ties up his son, and lays him on the wood.

When he takes the knife and raises his hand ready to strike, God speaks through an angel. Once again, God calls Abraham and blocks his hand. God recognizes his obedience and acknowledges that Abraham had not "withheld his son, his only son." He then allows Abraham to have his son back, and a ram is sacrificed instead of Isaac.

The story of Abraham being put to the test is a powerful reflection on absolute faith, trust, and obedience to the God whose ways are not our ways, according to the words of the prophet Isaiah (55:8). In the Christian tradition, it is seen as prefiguring the death of Jesus on the cross. It will be represented many times in art and literature.

The death of Abraham

This is the length of Abraham's life, one hundred seventy-five years.
Abraham breathed his last and died in a good old age, an old man
and full of years, and was gathered to his people.

After the death of Abraham God blessed his son Isaac. And Isaac
settled at Beer-lahai-roi.

(Genesis 25:7–8, 11)

Now the Book of Genesis presents the end of Abraham's life and begins to focus on his son, Isaac. After Abraham's inheritance passes to Isaac, he dies "full of years" (an expression meaning "fullness of life and goodness"), and he "was gathered to his people."

The long story of Isaac, marked by the blessing of God, now begins. That precious golden thread continues to connect the centuries and generations all the way to Jesus and, with him, to me and to you—to us.

Isaac

us

Jesus

Gianfranco Ravasi

was born in Merate in the northern region of Lombardy near Milan, Italy, in 1942 and was ordained a priest in 1966. For many years, he served as prefect of the Ambrosian Library in Milan and taught Old Testament exegesis at the Theological Faculty of Northern Italy in Milan as well as Hebrew in the archdiocesan seminary of Milan. In 2007, Pope Benedict XVI appointed him president of the Pontifical Council for Culture and also named him president of the Pontifical Commissions for the Cultural Heritage of the Church and of Sacred Archeology. In 2010, the same pope made him a cardinal. Over his long career, he published numerous books. This is his first children's book.

Silvia Colombo

lives and works in Brianza, in the northern region of Lombardy, Italy. After dedicating herself to nature illustrations, she fulfilled her lifelong dream of using vibrant colors to illustrate fairy tales and legends to charm children and adults alike. She currently works for various publishers and children's magazines.

Originally published in Italian as *Il Viaggio di Abramo*
©Edizioni San Paolo s.r.l, 2014
Piazza Soncino, 5 – 20092 Cinisello Balsamo (Milano)
www.edizionisanpaolo.it

Translation copyright © 2015 by Paulist Press. Translated by Bret Thoman.

Library of Congress Control Number: 2015942942

ISBN 978-0-8091-6775-3 (hardcover)
ISBN 978-1-58768-555-2 (e-book)

English-language edition published by

Paulist Press
997 Macarthur Boulevard
Mahwah, New Jersey 07430

www.paulistpress.com

Printed and bound in the
United States of America
by Versa Press, East Peoria, IL
August 2015